Positive Discipline for Kids

How to Listen Your Kids and Help Them to Develop Self-Discipline, Raise Confident and Positive Discipline in Life

Written By

Jack Dowson & Sara Dowson

© **Text Copyright 2019 by Jack Dowson & Sara Dowson!**

All rights reserved. No part of this guide may be reproduced in any form without permission in writing from the publisher except in the case of brief quotations embodied in critical articles or reviews.

Legal & Disclaimer

The information contained in this book and its contents is not designed to replace or take the place of any form of medical or professional advice; and is not meant to replace the need for independent medical, financial, legal or other professional advice or services, as may be required. The content and information in this book has been provided for educational and entertainment purposes only.

The content and information contained in this book has been compiled from sources deemed reliable, and it is accurate to the best of the Author's knowledge, information and belief. However, the Author cannot guarantee its accuracy and validity and cannot be held liable for any errors and/or omissions. Further, changes are periodically made to this book as and when needed. Where appropriate and/or necessary, you must consult a professional (including but not limited to your doctor, attorney, financial advisor or such other professional advisor) before using any of the suggested remedies, techniques, or information in this book.

Upon using the contents and information contained in this book, you agree to hold harmless the Author from and against any damages, costs, and expenses, including any legal fees potentially resulting from the application of any of the information provided by this book. This disclaimer applies to any loss, damages or injury caused by the use and application, whether directly or indirectly, of any advice or information presented, whether for breach of contract, tort, negligence, personal injury, criminal intent, or under any other cause of action.

You agree to accept all risks of using the information presented inside this book.

You agree that by continuing to read this book, where appropriate and/or necessary, you shall consult a professional (including but not limited to your doctor, attorney, or financial advisor or such other advisor as needed) before using any of the suggested remedies, techniques, or information in this book.

Positive Discipline for Kids

Table of Contents

Introduction 13
Chapter 1: Why Positive Discipline? 15
    The idea behind the positive discipline: 16
    Building a healthy relationship: 16
    Improved the kid's behavior: 17
    Learn to control: 18
    Learn about the world: 18
    • Some Basic Concept /Positive Discipline and Your Preschooler 19
    Basic criteria for positive discipline: 19
    Sense of connection: 20
    Encouraging and respectful: 20
    Long-term effective: 20
    Teaches significant social and life skills: 21
    Provide them opportunities: 21
    Positive discipline tactics and your preschooler: 22
    Reinforcement of positive actions: 23
    Consequences: 24
    Extinction: 25
    Rewards: 26
    Distraction and redirection: 27

Time in or time out 27

Take away facilities: 28

Chapter 2: Personality: How yours affects theirs .. 29

Watch your actions 30

Do not find the easy escape 30

Make them reasoning 31

Understanding Developmental Appropriateness 32

Best curriculum design strategy: 32

Every children's need is different: 33

Role of a teacher: 33

Flexible method: 34

Students keep themselves active: 34

•The Miraculous Brain: In learning and Development 35

Strong observation: 35

Strong 5 senses: 36

Learn to react: 36

The growth of Child's brain ability: 37

Excellent memory: 38

Strategies to enhance brain function in learning and development: 38

Active their mind: 38

Social gatherings: 39

Deal him according to his age: 40

Be gentle: 40

Talking time: 41

Chapter 3: I Can Do: The Joys (and Challenges) of Initiative: 42

Start believing in himself: 42

Utilizing his energy in a positive way: 43

To make their own future: 43

The approach of a parent and teacher: 44

Encourage them to do it: 44

Set examples for them: 45

Praise the effort not the results: 45

Accepting the Child You Have: Understanding Temperament 45

Characteristics of temperament: 47

Activity level: 47

Sensitivity: 48

Regularity: 49

Approach and withdrawal: 49

Adaptability: 50

Intensity: 50

Mood: 51

Attention span: 51

Responsiveness threshold: 51

• "Don't Talk to Me in That Tone of Voice". Emotions & the art of communication: 52

Impact of high voice tone or yelling: 53

Ignore it: 53

Losing the message 53

Damaged the relationship between kid and parent: .. 54

Emotions and art of communication with kids: 54

• Why Does My Child Do That?" : The messages of Misbehavior: 55

Attention: 56

He needs something: 56

A child suffering from depression: 57

Lack of information: 57

Chapter 4: Mistaken Goals at Home 59

Power: 59

Attention: 60

Inadequacy: 60

Revenge: 61

Strategies to redirect behavior: 61

Check your behavior and emotion: 62

Listen and understand what your kid is trying to say:62

Understand the need of your kid: 63

- Mistaken goals in the preschool 63

Mistaken goals and feelings: 64

Behavior is a mere thing: 65

- "You Can't Come to My Birthday Party: Social Skills for Preschoolers: 66

Vital Social skills for preschoolers: 66

Sharing: 67

Caring: 68

Communication: 68

Listening: 69

Group activities: 70

Chapter 5: Ending Bedtime Battles: Preschoolers and Sleep 71

Setting up the sleeping routine 72

Issues that can create trouble in preschooler sleeping 73

Parents role in healthy eating habits 75

Encourage good eating habits 75

When to start toilet training? 78

How to involve kids in toilet training? 79

Selecting (and Living with) Child Care 81

Look around critically 81

Check the policy 82

Always keep a check on services 82

Always keep yourself open for choices 82

Be interactive with staff.. 83

Trust your intuition 83

Chapter 6: Family and Class Meetings for Preschoolers 85

Why to work on the class meetings with kids? 86

Why family class meetings for preschoolers? 86

Benefits of class meetings 87

The World "Out There": Dealing with the Influence of Technology and Culture 88

Preschool learning and impact of technology.......... 89

Parenting and culture 89

Technology and kids learning................................... 90

Chapter 7: When your Child Needs Special help ... 92

Unable to focus 93

Having sleep issues... 93

Health is not on a good note 94

Unable to express.. 94

Mixed feelings of anger, excitement and sorrow 95

Growing as a Family: Finding Support, Resources, and Sanity 95

Your support is the key... 97

Hit the help resources 98

Medical attention 98
Additional attention 99
Discussion and debate 100
Educational grooming... 100
Getting study kits 101
Understand the variation.................................... 101
Explore the options 102
Match interests... 102
Participate to make it rational 103
Boost your kid's confidence 104
Make him realization of variation 105
Learn the best way to deal with it...................... 106

Chapter 8: Positive Discipline Solutions A-Z 107
Sibling rivalry 107
School problems 108
Eating preferences 108
Tatting and Lying 109
And more 109
Pro tip 110
Work On Magic Wands, Being Human, Reconnection & Change 110
Magic wands 111
Being human 111

Reconnection 112
  Bringing change 112
Conclusion 114

Introduction

Kids are the future of the nation and the family as well. It is important to make them learn the best codes of life that will help them to be successful. Discipline is one of the crucial and critical components of success in life. It is not just about the understanding of right or wrong but letting a child to adopt some specific regulations in life. Mannerism, dignity, public dealing, respecting others, behaving sanely, following laws and progress economically and socially are the products a person can have from the discipline.

To make our kids successful in future it is necessary to invest our time and efforts in their present. Positive discipline development in kids can help them to set specific rules and codes for their life. In addition to that, they will be more confident, positive and optimistic in life, school, home and social relations. For you to know more about the positive discipline and how to help your child with it we got you covered in this book.

This book on Positive discipline learning for the child is not just covers the basic topics of the mannerism and behaviors. It focuses on the complex behaviors, critical emotions, social and psychological challenges as well. the need to understand diversity among kids and its importance is highlighted in the book. Parents can get the answers about the questions related to reconnect kids to humanity and nature.

Chapter 1: Why Positive Discipline?

Most of the parents like you are struggling to handle their kid's behavior. Most of them complained about the negative behavior of their toddlers. For solving the issue of their child's behavior, some parents joined the parenting classes. On the other hand, a few of them start to read the guides to resolve this issue. Handling the children at the early stage is undoubtedly very crucial and sensitive matter.

If you are a new parent then I can understand it is tough for you. Within weeks and months, the baby who was in your lap started to crawl. In addition, after some more time he started to walk and created a mess. On some of his mistakes, you want to shout, hit, and punish him. But you know what? You do not need to harm or hit him to control his bad behavior. You can handle his behavior with positive discipline.

The idea behind the positive discipline:

The positive discipline was designed on the idea that kids are not bad. But their behavior is bad. It highlights only the positive aspects of kid behavior. In fact, with this strategy parents and teachers can teach good behavior to kids. On the other hand, it can eliminate bad behavior with time.

For changing your kid's bad behavior, adopt the positive discipline strategy. According to a famous saying, reach a child's heart rather than its head. The meaning of this saying is that deal him with love and compassion. Positive discipline plays a key role in developing his personality.

The reasons why you should adopt positive discipline are mentioned below.

Building a healthy relationship:

Do you want to build a healthy relationship with your child? For this purpose, you need to treat him well. Your positive attitude will attract him to you. When you will listen to him that will encourage him to share his feelings with you. He will start trusting you and will look up to you. All these factors will help you to develop a healthy and trustworthy relationship with your kid.

Improved the kid's behavior:

A kid is looking for a connection since his birth. Positive discipline helps him to develop that connection with his family or teachers. Different studies showed that the kids who have that connection are less likely to misbehave. They indirectly learn from them that help them to develop their good behavior. The kids learn various social skills just because of the positive discipline.

Various psychological studies showed that most kids misbehaved to grab attention. If you are giving proper attention to your kid, he will not misbehave. Rather than misbehaving, he will try to act decently. In reality, it is not a kid's fault it is just his nature. In addition, every kid has this nature; your child is not exceptional. Therefore, try to develop that connection with your kid and give him proper attention.

Learn to control:

The positive discipline is also important for his self-control and limit. He learns which behavior is acceptable at home or at school. With this, he gradually starts to control him-self. He also understands that there is a limit. Parents should also restrict them in a positive sense. Do not let them do whatever they want.

To make them secure and protective parents need to draw some boundaries. If they will not do, that kid will have low self-control. In addition, in fact, this low self-control will become a big problem in future. They will get frustrated and on the other hand, their anger will increase.

Learn about the world:

The positive discipline approach allows you to give the space to a kid. He will make mistakes and will learn. It is important too. As a kid learns to stand and walk after falls, likewise he learns after mistakes. Set a boundary but within that protective boundary give him freedom.

• Some Basic Concept /Positive Discipline and Your Preschooler

The positive discipline is a program initiated by Alfred Adler and Rudolf Dreikurs. The objective of this program is to help your kids to become more responsible, and respectful. Besides that, it also helps them to become useful members of society. For both kids and parents, positive discipline is effective. Both learn social and life skills in an encouraging and respectful manner. Parents without verbal and physical abuse can handle their child perfectly with this program.

Basic criteria for positive discipline:

For positive discipline, you need to follow the criteria. As a parent or a teacher, you need to fall on this. It is divided into 5 parts and each part has its own significance. These five criteria for positive discipline are:

Sense of connection:

At the first stage, you need to help your kid is having a feeling of connection. He can relate to you and can feel his belonging with you without any fear. This connection must be strong and significant.

Encouraging and respectful:

The extreme of anything can be harmful. Similarly, your extreme kindness or firmness can be dangerous for the kid. You need to be kind and firm both, at the same time. It will be encouraging and respectful for both the parents and kids.

Long-term effective:

A child has a limited canvas, as he does not know about the outer world. For stopping him or reacting to his mistake, you need to think. If you will think before reacting, you will get long-term effective results. For getting, long-term effects place you in the kid's situation. Go into his position and state of mind. In addition, think what you will do if you will be at his place. What you need to do to stop him from the same activity in future.

Teaches significant social and life skills:

For positive discipline, teach him all the significant social and life skills with love. These include concern for others and respect, cooperation or helping others, and solving the problems with courage. Also, teach them the skills to contribute to the school or society in a healthy way. In other words, all the qualities required for a strong and good character.

Provide them opportunities:

Provide the kids opportunities so that they can discover their capabilities. Encourage them to use their energy in a constructive way.

Positive discipline tactics and your preschooler:

To handle a preschooler is an everyday challenge for both, parents and teachers. It is a very sensitive age for the kids. They feel small things and actions deeply. For sopping the kid from misbehaving sometimes, parents get harsh. They do not think about the consequences of their harsh behavior. Mostly parents mixed the term discipline with the punishment. Both of them are in different terms.

To protect a kid's self-esteem and to build their confidence positive discipline tactics are the key. These tactics are useful for parents at home and teachers at school. With these tactics, you can handle the kid in a smooth way without hurting him. Remember one thing; every kid is different from the other. Therefore, for different kids different tactics are effective. Try one or more than one tactic for developing good behavior in your kid.

Reinforcement of positive actions:

To remember anything its reinforcement is important even for adults. Similarly, for kids reinforcement of positive behavior or actions is the must. Various studies showed that a kid needs appreciation for his positive acts from parents. With this appreciation, the kid motivated to do good things. You will see a positive change in your kid's behavior.

Moreover, it is also important to ignore his negative actions. Do not reinforce his negative actions by recalling them. In case, if you cannot ignore it than deal it with patience. Sit with your kid and explain to him why you are stopping him from that action. Communication with your kid is very important. You can stop him by explaining to him rather than humiliating him.

The specific behavior of a kid will strengthen that will get parental attention. It is the perception of Latham and you will observe it. A kid needs parent's attention whether it is in a good way or bad. It is suggested to completely ignore the bad or negative behavior of the kid.

Consequences:

A kid faces consequences on each behavior. Some consequences are natural while some are logical consequences. Both of these consequences have a strong impact on the kid. The natural consequence includes the reaction that happens automatically. On the other hand, logical consequence includes the reaction of parents.

Here are two examples of natural consequences. One is an injury as the result of a fight with an elder sibling. Another example of this is a toy breaking when kid throws it in anger on the floor. To understand the logical consequence here is the example. A kid did not get the toy for a day because of a fight with siblings.

Experts believe that natural consequences are not preferable. Because it can put the kid in danger. They also suggested that logical consequences should not be harsh. The best approach of logical consequence is to warn the kid before the action.

Extinction:

If you are not appreciating kid's good behavior, it means you extinct it. Your ignorance leads the kid towards disappointment. He stops doing that certain good action. Yes, you need to ignore his bad actions to stop him from doing that again. However, it is not the same in the case of good behavior or action.

According to Severe, a researcher it is devastating for your kid. Your ignorance will weaken your kid's positive behavior. When a kid's good behavior goes unnoticed, it gives him a feeling that it was not worthy. Therefore, he did not continue that specific action. Thus, must appreciate or reward your kid on his positive behavior.

Rewards:

For kids, motivation and rewards played the role of fuel. Rewards matters a lot for kids. They become happy with small things. You do not need to spend a lot of money on buying rewards for him. Only a small star, a hug, and a kiss can make him happy. Whenever he did something good, give him a reward.

With this strategy, you can also stop him from bad behavior. Ask him to stop doing an unacceptable thing and you will give him reward. If he has, done something exceptional present him a toy. On small things, give him a reward. If you do not have, stars just draw it with a pen on his hand. You can adopt this strategy for improving his overall behavior.

Some experts criticize this technique. According to them, this strategy stops the kid from learning. He does everything in the lust of the gift or reward. The experts urge that it is not good for his long-term personality development. In addition to this, there are experts who believe it is an exceptional tactic.

Distraction and redirection:

Distraction and redirection is a useful tactic to help your kid. Most of the experts suggested this technique. You can easily convert the kid's attention from bad behavior. It will help the kid to forget that certain bad action. Whenever a kid starts to misbehave, engage him in any creative activity.

If you will stop the kid by force, he will be frustrated. He will shout and can be emotionally disturbed. Therefore, the best solution to deal with this is to distract him from that action. It will also help you too from bearing his tantrums even at public places.

Time in or time out

Time in or time out is an instant reaction to unacceptable behavior. It can be given after a serious negative behavior like hitting someone. However, for this parents should warn the kid prior to this. Different experts have different opinions on this tactic. Some believe that it is an effective tactic.

Kid faces the consequences on the spot and can understand that he has something bad. On the other hand, some experts are against it. They believe that this strategy abandons the kid.

Take away facilities:

Taking away facilities or privileges is different from logical consequences. You opt this action on unacceptable behavior. It is the last option or tactic to bring the kid on right track. When parents feel that there is no room expect this than they opt for this tactic.

As every kid has a different nature so treat every kid differently. You need to go to his level. Try to understand first the reason behind his bad behavior. Understand his feelings and then take action.

Chapter 2: Personality: How yours affects theirs

For kids their parents are the live example and guideline. The very first role model of a kid is his or her mother and father. The kids observe how their parents are dealing with the people, issues, matter and routine work as well. Other than the actions, your personal traits and personality do affect the kid and a kind of model for them.

Before getting started with how your personality affects theirs, it is necessary to know what defines your personality. Personality is the combination of behavior, reaction, treatment to situation and public dealing. If as a parent you are kind to others and have polite nature the kid will definitely learn the politeness and kindness though observation. Same as on the other hand if you have anger issues or mostly confused in the decision making or taking a stance then your child will end up with the same condition.

When it comes to make your kid learn the positive discipline, you need to work on the overall discipline as well. Something you want your kids to learn you are supposed to do the same in front of them. As per the recent study of behavioral learning explains that kids are good at observation and the visuals they have in daily life are the biggest source for them to learn everything. From the manners to behaviors and even the way of life, they learn from the environment and elders.

Watch your actions

If you want to bring change in your kid, the most important thing is to watch your actions. If you are lying to your kids, they will lie back to you. This is something that is learning from your behavior and action in the first place. You are supposed to give them reasons for everything that is happening.

Do not find the easy escape

Scolding a child on questions, giving lame excuses or ignore their questions is the easy escape that parents have most of the time. This is something that can lead to the adverse behavioral changes in the kids. They will adopt the habit or ignorance and anger when they are unable to sort out the problem or do not have answers.

Make them reasoning

If there is something, you are unable to do for the kids or some things are impossible or unmanageable then you are supposed to reason that. When you give solid and measureable reasons for something that develop a habit and understanding of logic in the kid. They will know the way to say not is proper reasoning not just running away. It seems to be a difficult task in the beginning but eventually you can make some real improvement in your kid's behavior and overall discipline as well.

Understanding Developmental Appropriateness

Developmental appropriateness is an approach to teach the kid. In this approach, the curriculum designed according to the age and his individual needs. The basic objective of this program is that every kid fits in this program. In other words it is a program for each kid. He should not need to fit in the program as the program will fit in him.

Best curriculum design strategy:

Designing the curriculum for preschoolers is a critical task. A teacher needs to keep various elements in mind. The development appropriate strategy helps the teacher to design the best curriculum. With reference to this approach curriculum designed according to the capabilities of a student. At a certain age what he can do physically, cognitively, and emotionally. This strategy helps in all these perspectives.

Every children's need is different:

The teachers of preschool look at the whole child individually. They see his physical, intellectual, emotional, social and creative growth. The growth of these different segments raised in every child at its own speed. Some factors developed in some children at early stage. On the other side, in some children, they develop later.

Every child has capabilities but teachers need to recognize and polish them. Some preschoolers have strong intellectual skills. But he needs to develop those skills through socialization. Likewise some kids have great speaking power. However, the only thing they need is confidence to speak in public. Besides this there are some common developmental patterns that are there too, same for all kids.

Role of a teacher:

Through the developmentally appropriate approach teacher observe all the preschooler's behavior. By utilizing her experience she will recognize the capabilities of students. According to their strength teachers design and plan the activities. She tried that those activities should not be too easy or too tough for kids. The purpose of these activities is to help students to grow and learn.

Flexible method:

To make it feasible for all the student's development appropriate approach has flexible methods. These methods are open-ended and have limited chances of mistakes. The reason behind this strategy is to teach all the kids equally. With the fewer chances of mistakes, students learn with confidence.

Students keep themselves active:

For a child's positive discipline it is important that he remains busy in positive activities. The development appropriation keeps the kid busy. If your preschooler is engaged in his own independent activities it is a sign. Yes, it is a sign of his appropriate development. He will not get frustrated, or bored. Rather than that he will engage in the activities his teacher taught him.

•The Miraculous Brain: In learning and Development

Your child has a miraculous brain like other kids. Even before birth till age 5, child's brain develops with the highest speed. The brain development at early age has a long-lasting impact on his ability to learn. This early learning remains with him for the rest of life. His early childhood's positive or negative experiences play a key role in his brain development.

Strong observation:

The observation of a child at an early age is very strong. His brain picks up the information and actions at an incredible pace. His brain process that observation speedily and he connects all his observations with previous observations.

He observes people around him and their behavior towards them. Along this he observes his physical environment. For instance colors, food, fabric patterns, sounds, roof, walls, and so on. These observations play an important role in his early development and learning.

Strong 5 senses:

The miraculous brain keeps all his 5 senses super active. His listening, speaking, seeing, tasting, and touching, all senses are really strong at this age. From a normal person, their brain absorbs more than these senses. His senses make him extra sensitive, especially about his physical environment. With these multiple strong senses, he learns various things in a short time.

Learn to react:

As a child's brain works efficiently he learns to react. Since the birth of a child he starts his journey to learn how to react. When he should laugh or cry. How to tell he is hungry or in pain? He starts to understand the feelings of joy or sadness. Similarly, he reacts to the situations. He learns who is her mother or to whom he feels protective? He learns all these reactions and feelings at a high speed through amazing brain functions.

The growth of Child's brain ability:

According to the studies initial years are really important for a kid's learning. You are thinking how he digests lots of information at the same time. Yes, you are thinking right because adults mostly can't digest more information at a time. But a kid's brain works differently. You will be surprised by the kid's brain ability development process.

A kid's brain ability not decreased but increased with increasing information. With the increased information he started to connect and relate it with the previous information. It expands his imagination and learning canvas.

Excellent memory:

At early stage of life a kid has an excellent memory. He observes things and saved them in his brain. He tried to copy the actions of people around him. Most of the kids didn't forget anything that they see only once. Therefore, it is important for parents to behave well when kids are around them.

Strategies to enhance brain function in learning and development:

As mentioned earlier every child has a miraculous brain. But the pace of learning of each child will be different from others. If you feel that your kid is going at a slow pace don't worry. You and her teachers can deal with it. There are some strategies that will enhance his brain function to help him.

Active their mind:

If you see your kid is not properly acting help him in activating his mind. You can do this by engaging him in different healthy physical activities. These activities must be interesting and should be designed according to the kid's age. Must try to make them not too simple or too hard. Talk to his teacher and design an activity jointly. So that he can do this in school and at home.

Social gatherings:

Man is a social animal and can't live without others. Similarly, kids also need to socialize for their development and mental growth. Take them to the parks and allow them to socialize with the kids. It will help them to make friends. On the other hand his sadness or depression will vanish. You will observe the positive change in your kid's behavior with this simple action.

Besides eliminating his sadness he will learn positive discipline. He will learn to share, cooperate, and to help others. In schools, teachers arrange parties or social gatherings just because of its positive impact.

Deal him according to his age:

You need to deal the child according to his age. If he is 3 years old and you feel he is weak in counting. Don't worry. Just leave him for some time. 4 years is the age when child's brain cortex formed. That's the point that you were looking for. It is best for mathematics and logic.

At this age gently start to encourage him to count. Give him small activities like collecting the objects. Likewise labeling and comparing different objects. Teach him while playing. Don't force him and don't get angry. He will learn sometimes within minutes or sometimes within days.

Be gentle:

For kid's brain development and learning, your anger can be destructive. Kids only need your attention and love, whether you are a parent or teacher. Kids are sensitive in nature thus, handle them with care and be gentle. It is possible he will take some time in learning but it's ok. He is a child.

Put yourself in his position or level and see what you will do?

Talking time:

It is really important that your kid talks to you. If he is in school he talks to his peers. Let him talk for some time. You can't imagine the positives of this talking on your kid's learning and development. First, they get the confidence to share their feelings with you and teachers. Secondly, during their talk, they learn something from their talking partner. It can be a new word, a gesture, or anything else.

Chapter 3: I Can Do: The Joys (and Challenges) of Initiative:

A kid has to do various new things on a daily basis. For learning new things he takes initiatives. As a parent or teacher you need to appreciate and encourage him. He looks up to you before taking a step. As a parent when you feel happy when your kid takes first step. Similarly a kid also feels happy when he does something first time. For him it is like conquering a mountain. Therefore, appreciate him.

Every initiative comes with challenges or obstacles. These hurdles are part of life and a learning process. But for kids these hurdles are really disappointing. Give them the courage that they can do it. As a parent you can do this. The behavior of taking initiatives helps the kid to spend his life with optimism.

Start believing in himself:

With initiatives, a kid starts to believe in himself. He helps to develop his childhood through different experiments. It also helps him in developing relationships with others. Because he believes in himself and it gives him confidence to initiate talking.

Utilizing his energy in a positive way:

For initiating anything a kid needs courage and energy to execute it. Thus, the kids who initiate new things spend their positive energy on them. It also protects them from bad behavior. As they concentrate totally on positive things.

To make their own future:

Taking initiatives helps a lot in kid's positive youth development. Taking initiative at an early age demands courage and strength. If a kid is taking it in his childhood it means he is courageous. His future will also be bright. He will not be afraid of taking initiatives and risks at any part of his life. Further, he will deal with the problems and hurdles that will come to stop him.

The approach of a parent and teacher:

For encouraging your kid to take initiative you need to adopt a few ways. These ways will help you or the teacher to teach the kid to take initiative. Give him confidence so that he can say that yes, I can do this. Further, he can enjoy the joy of the initiatives. And on the other hand, he can face the challenges comes in its way.

Encourage them to do it:

At the initial stage, a kid needs support from you and in school from teachers. Kids have abilities beyond our expectations. Thus, encourage them and give them confidence. Give them space and provide opportunities. Let them do it what they can and want to initiate. With this they will get the experience doing something practically. With this they will come to know the difference between seeing something and doing it.

Set examples for them:

Rather than forcing him to do something, set an example for him. Setting an example will encourage him more than saying. Kids look up to you for doing anything. They tried to copy their parents and teachers. Do those actions in front of the kid you want him to do.

Praise the effort not the results:

Before criticizing the kid remember one thing. He is a kid. Never judge him on the results of an action. You should appreciate him for his efforts. For us that nothing but for kid it was really tough. So, appreciate him for his courage and effort.

Accepting the Child You Have: Understanding Temperament

As a parent accept your kid with his behavior whether it's good or bad. You need to understand his temperament to raise him as a confident and well-disciplined kid. Everyone has temperaments, even adults and elders.

But handling the kid and understanding his temperaments are really important.

Temperament is a kid's way of thinking, reacting or behaving on a specific thing. For parents and teachers, it is essential to understand the kid's temperament. Along this it is also significant to understand their own temperaments too. As this understanding will make parenting easy and effective for parents.

Temperament is not in the hands of a child. He didn't choose to have temperaments. Researches showed that it has neurological, physiological, and biological factors. Because of those factors a kid reacts to a situation or affects his mood. Whether these temperaments are right or wrong it's not a child's fault. Moreover, your yelling or hitting the kid is not going to change his temperament.

Characteristics of temperament:

According to the researchers there are nine characteristics of temperaments. All these factors are important as all of them have their own significance. These factors also show how your kid will fit in the school. His temperament affects how he does his homework and activities at home.

Activity level:

The activity level means how much your kid is physically active. Running, moving, and jumping, playing, and other such things. Compared his active time period with his inactive time period. When he is engaging in an activity but not doing it with full energy. Kids have either high energy or low energy.

For the kids with active energy, it is difficult to fit in school environment. Because in school environment he has to sit for long hours. His restlessness can also cause disturbance for other kids in the class. For such kids teachers and parents need to channelize the energy. You can benefit the kid and also can maintain the discipline in the class.

On the other hand, the kids who have low energy settled well in the class. But sometimes they seem unmotivated. Mostly, they sit in the class peacefully but seem not interested in the class activities.

Sensitivity:

The second factor of understanding the temperament is sensitivity. Your kid can easily be affected by the change in environment. Moreover, there are countless factors that can easily distress him.

For example, a chair can be hard for him and his clothes may cause itching. Change in the weather can also cause cold. These kids are sensitive in nature. And it has a negative effect on his academics and personality. While kids with less sensitivity are more tolerant of environment.

Regularity:

Regularity in kid's daily activities has an impact on the kid's temperament. Such as his routine of eating, or walking. Parents should observe the after-school routine of a preschooler. Every kid has different patterns and habits.

For kids with high regularity, change is very difficult. They get along well in the classroom but face problems in outdoor activities. On the other side, kids with low regularity cannot stay in one place. Therefore, they feel hard to fit in the class. Because they cannot follow the same routine for long time. Besides that they also create trouble for their peers and teachers.

Approach and withdrawal:

The first reaction of your kid to a new situation. Kids with a bolder approach welcome new experiences due to their curious nature. While the kids who are shy are hesitant towards the new things. They never attracted towards new situation at first glance. They take their time in observing and then accept it slowly.

Adaptability:

Every child doesn't adopt new changes or situations easily. Few kids need time to get familiar with the new circumstances. On the other hand, few kids adapt changes easily. Sometimes, kids who adopt the changes easily can put themselves in danger. Because they can trust and depend on anyone. While the slow adopter kids get stressed and frustrated with new situations.

Intensity:

Intensity leads to the energy a kid spends on reacting to anything. Whether it's positive or a negative reaction. Kids with high reaction intensity react with full power. On the opposite side, the low reaction intensity kids come. They are less expressive and in most of the situations they keep silent.

Mood:

A kid's mood changed in seconds. Kids have a variety of emotions. Sometimes as a parent you didn't understand his moods. It is important for you to understand his emotions and moods. In most of the situations few kids remain in good moods. But in reality they do not understand and deal his emotions honestly.

Attention span:

Kids rather have short and high attention spans. It is the time that a child spends on an activity. If he is spending more time on an activity means he is a high attention span. Such kids never get frustrated or disappointed easily. On the other hand, kids with short attention span get tired. They get frustrated and give up easily.

Responsiveness threshold:

This characteristic of temperament leads towards the stimulation your kid needs to the response. It can be a sound, posture, or other such things. Highly responsive children react to various things within seconds. These things include sound, smell, taste, touch and etc. On the other side the low responsive doesn't move on things easily.

• "Don't Talk to Me in That Tone of Voice". Emotions & the art of communication:

It's a child's universal right that his voice needs to be heard. Along this, it must be taken seriously. Communication is equally important for the kid as it is for the adults. While talking with kids parents usually used non-verbal communication. But on a kid your gestures, body language, and voice tone all have a huge impact.

As you don't like that someone talks to you in a harsh tone. Likewise is the case with kids they also get disturbed with your voice tone. Your calm voice will make your kids calmer. Do you want to know a golden rule of parenting? Stay calm when your kid has done something wrong. Some parents complain that they want to calm but they lost it.

Impact of high voice tone or yelling:

Yelling has a negative impact on your kid. It totally shatters his personality. Besides that he becomes more aggressive and misbehaved.

Ignore it:

When a parent yells at the kid he totally ignores it. There are various studies that showed this. Kids never give importance to listening to what you are saying while yelling.

Losing the message

While yelling a kid can only focus on your voice tone. The message you want to convey through yelling he totally loosed it. The reason for this is not intentional. Unintentionally he missed the message due to the loud voice.

Damaged the relationship between kid and parent:

Yes, voice tone damaged the relationship between kids and parents. He will start to avoid you. Moreover, he will start to be afraid of you. It will damage your relationship with the kid badly.

Emotions and art of communication with kids:

Communicating with the kids in art. You need to teach them the communication through which they can express their emotions. Teach them sign language if they can't read or talk properly. It will help you to understand your feeling. Talk with them in non-verbal communication so that they can understand it.

Kids like to be loved. With your hug, kiss, and other such gestures you can comfort them. It is also a way of communication. Through these signs, you can tell them that you care about them. Your love and compassion will make their self-esteem stronger.

And they will develop a strong and healthy relationship with you. It will also protect them from any negative behavior.

• Why Does My Child Do That?" : The messages of Misbehavior:

There is always a reason behind the misbehavior of a kid. You are seeing your kid misbehaving with others you need to take it seriously. Don't announce that your kid is misbehaving or is a bad boy. With this you kid's behavior will worsen rather than improving. Every kid has different attitude towards everything.

His every attitude has a cause. There must be something that is bothering him. Therefore, deal him gently. Don't shout on him. Sit with him and talk to him to find out the reason behind his behavior. The most common reasons that could be a cause of his misbehavior.

Attention:

A kid needs your proper attention. If you are ignoring him or not paying attention to him he will misbehave. And the reason for this misbehavior is to seek your attention. Kids like adults cannot express their feelings. Therefore, they use misbehavior as a tool of communication. They adopt this strategy to reach parents or their loved ones.

Try to understand his feelings. And analyze whether you or any other family member ignoring him. You need to address his issue. Spend some quality time with him and you will see improvement in his behavior.

He needs something:

Sometimes a kid misbehaved because he needs something important. It can be possible that he feels hungry or needs something to eat. Or maybe he needs a toy. If a child's desire or need never fulfilled he started to misbehave. As a parent, you need to notice his behavior and actions. Children are not mature enough to directly ask for something. You need to understand his needs with his gestures or actions.

A child suffering from depression:

Depression in kids? Yes, you will be surprised but it is true. Kids also have emotions and get stressed or frustrated about anything. When an action or situation bothered him he started to misbehave. As he cannot explain his feelings therefore, he hides behind the misbehavior. It's actually a reaction to his suffering. Therefore, support him with affection and try to identify the issue that is bothering him.

Lack of information:

Lack of information or limited information can also be a reason behind the kid's misbehavior. He got confused and puzzled while doing something for the first time. A kid cannot understand or learn after taking instructions only once. He needs to do that action repeatedly to get perfection in that action. As a parent or teacher you need to explain a thing at least trice.

Chapter 4: Mistaken Goals at Home

A kid who is misbehaving is actually trying to communicate with us. Because his needs whether it's physical or emotional are not fulfilling. The mistaken goal is a term referred to understand why students are misbehaving. When a kid feels that you are not fulfilling his needs he will turn to the "mistaken goals".

These goals are called mistaken. Yes, mistake because these are a try by the kid to get his desired thing. And there are four major mistaken goals that you will see in your kid. And the only reason behind this is to fulfill his need.

These mistaken goals are power, attention, inadequacy, and revenge.

Power:

Power is an important mistaken goal. A kid wants to be a boss and wants some space. If you are giving him too many instructions that can trigger this goal. In this case, firstly help him in understanding the situation. Secondly, encourage him to do what he is trying to do in your supervision.

Attention:

Is your kid is misbehaving with the goal of getting attention? Observe this when he is misbehaving. When you are around or not. Is he misbehaving with everyone or only with you? Analyze the situation. Think about it. Are you spending enough time with him or not. For a kid to measure your love towards him is the time. The much quality time you will spend with him means you love him.

If you really feel you kid is trying you to notice him pay attention. Spend extra time with him. With this, you will see a positive change in his behavior.

Inadequacy:

When your kid is tired of something or hopeless, he moves towards the inadequacy goal. In this goal a kid totally gives up and wants to be alone. He wants to disconnect himself from others. At that point as a parent your kid needs you the most. Tell him you are there for him and he can't give up.

Revenge:

When something hurts the kid in its reaction revenge goal emerges. Kids are sensitive anything can badly hurt them. It can be your harsh comment or anything. When he gets hurt he started to misbehave others. And the reason for this is to take revenge and to show his anger.

Strategies to redirect behavior:

As a parent, yelling or punishing is not the solution to control the kid's behavior. As these situations can escalate his behavior. There are three strategies or steps to redirect a kid's behavior.

Check your behavior and emotion:

As a parent, you need to check your own behavior and emotional status. Have you yelled at kid when you were stressed or tired? Have you negated him frequently? It is important to keep a check on yourself before reacting. If you are in stress and not available for him emotionally child's behavior will escalate. Therefore, it is important to redirect his behavior to make yourself emotionally available to him.

Listen and understand what your kid is trying to say:

Kids cannot describe their feelings in a clear way. You need to understand what he is trying to communicate. As a parent, it is a challenge for you to understand him. But unfortunately, in some cases parents get frustrated. That frustration has a negative effect on the kid's behavior. Thus, understand your kid's behavior goal and deal with it with affection and care.

Understand the need of your kid:

To understand the kid's feeling and needs is the most important task. Don't fulfill all their unnecessary needs. But at least listen to them. Show them you care for them. In a shopping center, the reason for their crying can be to get something. But one thing you are ignoring as you didn't listen to him. It can be another reason. Like he can be tired or hungry. Or maybe he is sleepy.

Therefore, to redirect the kid's behavior full-fill some needs. Besides that understand his unmet need and his feelings. Talk to him about that thing. Tell him the right and wrong about that thing. And yes, if you are doing promise to him fulfill it. Never break your promise and give him that thing as a gift on the promised day. With this he will trust you and on your promises.

• Mistaken goals in the preschool

These goals are associated with specific feelings. For example, a kid with loneliness might misbehave to gain attention. But the way of seeking tension can be unacceptable. Similarly, the reason behind an angry kid is to show he is powerful.

In preschool teachers, unfortunately, teachers also adopt these mistaken goals. As they think that they are powerful and right. And the kid is wrong and they can control him. But on the other side, kid also feels the same. He thinks he is right and he is strong enough to deal with the teacher.

This tussle between students and teachers creates a mess and unhealthy environment. You will not accept that you are wrong when you will be angry. Likewise, students also get frustrated and feel anxiety and shame.

Mistaken goals and feelings:

The basic mistaken goals that are connected with feelings. Like the mistaken goal "attention" is connected with loneliness or isolation. "Revenge, Power, and Control, who's right and who's wrong" is connected with anger. Besides this "Avoidance of failure" is connected with shame and anxiety. Similarly, Withdrawal-Avoidance-Relief is related to depression, guilt, shame, and anxiety.

It is important for a teacher to recognize the mistaken goals in students. And not only in students but also in themselves. Because only then they can deal with the students in a positive and healthy way.

Behavior is a mere thing:

Teachers should understand that behavior is not a problem. It is a mere thing. Deal it as a symptom, not as a serious problem. In other words, it is a reaction to a dysfunctional amount of emotions or thoughts. The only thing a student needs in that situation is your help. A teacher needs to keep student's history in front of him. And after proper observation and understanding she needs to handle it gently.

• "You Can't Come to My Birthday Party: Social Skills for Preschoolers:

Social skills are the skills we use to communicate and interact with others. On daily basis we met with the people and communicate with them. Similarly kids also meet with their peers and communicate with them. But it is also a fact that nowadays, even kids bully their peers. Based on their likes and dislikes they talk to their class fellows.

With coming to school kids start to make new friends. Some kids love to make friends. While on the other side some kids never want to talk to someone. They never want to talk to them and never share their things with them. It is very important to teach the kids social behavior through social skills in school. Because this training or learning will stay with him for the rest of his life.

Vital Social skills for preschoolers:

There are some vital and significant social skills. Parents need to reinforce them at home and teachers at school. Because reinforcement of these social skills is very important. You cannot teach these skills to kids. But yes you can reinforce these skills by showing it to them through your actions.

Sharing:

Sharing is an important skill. See whether your kid is sharing his toys or snacks willingly with his friends. There are various studies available on the sharing behavior of the kids. And these studies showed that from one to 3 years kids mostly share their things. But when they have stuff in quantity.

While from the age 3-6 kids are bit selfish and are possessive about their stuff. Especially when it comes to a thing that costs to themselves. For instance, if he has only one candy. And you asked him to share that candy, he will be reluctant. Sharing is important as it helps the kids to make new friends.

Develop the skills of sharing in your kid without using force. Give him incentives and appreciate him when he shares something with others. Make it a habit to reinforce him to share whenever there is an opportunity.

Caring:

For kids caring is an important social skill. From an early age, they need to learn compassion for their siblings and others. Teach the kids that when someone is in pain don't laugh as it is unacceptable. They need to help them whether it's a human being or an animal.

Communication:

The communication at the early stage of children is not proper. Most of the children hesitate to communicate. Even they avoid doing eye-contact with others while talking. It is important for them to have communication skills. As in their future it will help him in all aspects of life. He must know how to communicate with full confidence. He must use non-verbal communication appropriately.

In communication skills tell your child the difference between rude and polite communication. Teach them basic words at the age of 4 to 5. The words like thank you, sorry, and please. Make yourself a model for your kid. As at this stage, kids try to copy others rather than listening to you.

Listening:

Your kid's behavior, learning, positive discipline, everything depends on listening. Without listening skill a kid cannot learn anything. Besides that, he cannot excel in his life. A kid born with listening skills but you need to polish and enhance it.

To improve his listening skills you can play various games involving listening skill. For instance, whispering a word or telephone without bad signals. With these simple games you will see improvement in your kid's listening skills.

Group activities:

Teach the kids to engage in group activities. It will help him to work as a group member in his later age. As these are kids so design such games that can be played in a group. With this activity they will learn other things too. Like patience as they need to wait for their turn. They will listen to them carefully and will respect others.

Chapter 5: Ending Bedtime Battles: Preschoolers and Sleep

Sleep in an important factor and your kids especially preschoolers need around 11 to 12 hours' sleep should be added in their daily routine. So, it is important as a parent to develop good sleeping habits and make them prepare for the coming challenges. For parents it is quite a challenging thing to put a preschool on sleep, some moms and dads even lose their temper and impatient. Remember the kids follow the routine that set by their parents. So, to build an effective sleeping habits it is necessary to make your own habits in an appropriate way so the kids will follow you. When your preschooler takes enough sleep it will help to improve the overall health. It can improve the good mood, behavior grooming, physical and mental capabilities, enhance the focus and cognitive functions and eating habits as well.

Setting up the sleeping routine

Sleeping routine for preschooler is an effective and good for grooming or personality building. To set the sleeping habits you have to work on the bedtime routine for the preschooler. In a stick bedtime you just deliver a message and make their brain use to follow the particular task at a certain time. Here are some ways through which you can set a bedtime routine for preschooler:

- Bedtime routine is an effective way for preschooler to have enough required sleep.
- Try to make the bed room a quiet place, which is perfect to trigger the sleep.
- Finish the meal at least 2 hours before the bed time, and set the proper schedule for them includes playing, eating and for other activities.
- Develop a habit in them that the bed is just for sleep.
- Avoid the use of laptop, Tv or mobile at the time of sleep in bed room.

- Start giving them alerts 10 minutes before the bedtime, so their mind will act an alert that now to shut down other activities and prepare body to fall asleep.
- You can use the night time outfits to make an environment and communicate about its time to sleep.

Issues that can create trouble in preschooler sleeping

When it comes to making sleeping habits in preschooler remember what you instruct them and make them to do that habit will stay with them. Like a bedtime habit and napping, both helps to regain the energy and let them to perform even better throughout a day.

Sometimes due to any issue your preschooler can face the sleeping problem, like a bedtime nightmares or freighting in the dark may disturb their sleeping. To avoid such issue, it is good to create a bedroom environment equipped with their favorite stuff around that helps a lot to fall sleep early and stay with them on bed until they fell asleep. It gives them a sign of safety and security or in case of any serious issue you can consult with a specialist as well.

"I Don't Like That!": Preschoolers and Eating

In preschool stage kids usually like to make their own choices in eating and selection of food. They sometimes refuse the choice of parents to eat something. It is basically a stage of learning and exploring new things. So, it's good to develop a healthy food selecting habits in your kids at this time. This only be done by encouraging their choice and engage them in shopping. There are multiple other ways that can trigger the good eating habits in kids. At growing age healthy and balance diet is an essential requirement for your child's body. It will help you kids to be active throughout the day, provide multiple learning opportunities.

Parents role in healthy eating habits

Remember that parents play an important role in a=making good eating habits in their preschooler kids. They normally eat and prefer to try new things if the parents trying them. So, if you want that your l=kid must choose a specific food group in meal and avoid junks then you have to follow the same way in front of them. Try to give multiple healthy food choice in front of kids and do not put them in pressure to eat something and to not eat something. If your kid is refuse to eat the meal do not harsh or loud, as well as do not put pressure on them to eat or finish the food. On other hand split the food into different portions like breakfast, lunch or dinner and in between the meals add some healthy snacks options for the kid's choice.

Encourage good eating habits

For preschooler only parents can trigger the healthy eating habits with some effective ways. Here ae some useful things should consider:

- Offer the variety of food or healthy food choice in front of kids and let them allow to choose the one they want to have in meal.
- Make you own eating habits a bit modified, if you want that your kids have healthy and nutritional diet then first add it in your own diet.
- Make sure to provide the healthy food option and do not put the high calorie junk food in your house.
- Give your kids a privilege and importance to their choice as well. Like involve them in making food or take them on a shopping as well.
- Make a proper meal time plan for the kids to have their day meal with proper schedule. Whether it is breakfast, lunch or dinner even set the time for snacks as well. And adjust a suitable time difference between meals.
- Try to put them in the family gathering and share meals together at least on time

in a day. This will not only create a good environment but also provide a good atmosphere to have meals.

- Give the preschooler a control over to left the food if they feel full and satisfied. If your kid does not want to have any of the meal at the set time, then do not angry at all. It actually helps them to make the decision about to choose when they are hungry or when they are not.

Preschoolers and Potties: The Ongoing Saga of Toilet Training

Preschooler and potty training vary from child to child, not every kid is prepared to learn the basics about potty and to go toilet. It is necessary for the parents to understand and then put the kids into the learning procedure. Before starting the potty training it is necessary to make sure the kid is ready to learn and understand the basic instruction and know the difference of use of word potty.

Sometimes people concern that at the particular age kids will start understanding and ready to accept the training about how to use toilet. But as per the studies it is not related to the age it is about the signs that how quickly a kid will show you. All you need to understand the signs and start educating and give them training about it.

When to start toilet training?

Usually girls will learn earlier than boys about the word potty and learn the toilet techniques quickly. Parents need to put the focus on the following signs that should direct that now you have to start educating your kids about the toilet techniques.

- If you put diaper and see that it's still dry from about 2 to3 hours.
- If the kids showing interest in using the potty
- They understand the instructions and try to follow them.

Toilet training time period is varying from child to child. For some it's just a time of 3 months or may be 6 months but another way some kids will be able to learn then quickly. Parents can use the training pants as well for the toilet training. That can usually out at the night time and on the travelling. You found the pants are start continue to dry means now the kid is ready for the underwear instead of training pants.

How to involve kids in toilet training?

For the training or to put the kids into the understanding the potty and use of toilet it is necessary to use the word potty in front of them and make them recognize with the pee and pop. You can use the small and basic tips to involve them in process and make them to learn about.

- Communicate with the kids to tell when the diaper is wet
- Try to understand the kid's behavior about the urge to pee or pop and make them use to sit in a toilet with the help of a practicing chair.

- Not to enforce the kids to sit on the potty for the toilet practice if they are not willing to do it.
- You can set the timing or a routine about the pee or pop urge. Usually after 1 hour you have to take them out into a drill to sit on a potty.
- Try to read the face reading and understand the gesture to find out that your kid is in urge to go to toilet or sit on a potty.
- Train the kids to undress themselves before sitting on a potty, during training you have to be patience that they are in learning process and as a parent do not need to be aggressive on them.

During the potty training sometimes accidents may happen, but you have to keep yourself calm and do not stress out the kid as well. Because it is quite normal in potty learning in stressful situation sometime brain responses are quite different and even your potty trained can face the problems. But if you found the issues are serious you can consult with the health consultant as well.

Selecting (and Living with) Child Care

Parents who have their professional commitments usually look for the daycare and child cares services for the kids. Before choosing the one it is necessary to look in to the quality, professional, creative and hygienic environment. No matter the child care is a home based, professional place, private entity or a family base child care, here are some selecting tips that will help a lot to choose an appropriate one.

Look around critically

When you are going to check a child care services, it is necessary to look into their website critically. You should evaluate the atmosphere they are providing to kids, staff behavior and interaction with the kids as well as the staff ratio available at the child care to attend the kids. In initial age according to the authorities one person can enough to handle three infants or toddlers at a time but not more than that.

Check the policy

For the best child care services, you have to keep a check on the policy they have to treat child at different stages. Ask them and check their policy about putting babies on sleep, their eating or feeding and policy to treat the sick child. For the infants a family child care is an appropriate option.

Always keep a check on services

If you just hire child care services, then do not just rely and leave the things unchecked. You have to off and on visit the place and try to find out what kind of facilities they are providing to the kids and how much they intended to upgrade it. A child care does not mean that all the kids are at one place. Choose the one where they have separate room or space for the toddlers, infants and big kids.

Always keep yourself open for choices

Do not consider the one option is an ultimate one that now you cannot change the child care services.

Be open yourself for the best services. Like if you found something not good and you are not satisfied then it is an appropriate to just shift to another best options. So always have a backup option and keep looking for the best for your kid.

Be interactive with staff

Infant is not able to speak up about the things or communicate about the feelings. As a parent it is necessary to keep yourself up-to-date and interactive with the staff. You have to tell the staff about the kid home routine and always connected with the attended to know about what your kid is doing or he is going well or not.

Trust your intuition

It is a natural feeling that parents get the intuition about their kids if anything does not go well. If you found something bad in your gut, then do trust on that feeling and try to figure it out. It really helps to evaluate the wants of your kid and if found something bad then do not waste time to move for the best child care or a personal baby sitter option in town.

Chapter 6: Family and Class Meetings for Preschoolers

Class meeting activity for preschooler is an effective thing that helps to build the interactive skills in kids. As well as it is a learning source for them to improve the social behavior. According to the research it is evaluated that the purpose of the early meetings is to make the environment interactive. In this atmosphere kids are feel free to share their emotions and feelings which play a constructive role in their routines. Sometimes in these meetings the family or parents are also involve to make the interaction more useful. For the grooming and personality development these drills are impressive and helps to build confidence. Kids can make a better social interaction and an opportunity of growth and development, as well as can make friends or able to resolve their conflicts.

Why to work on the class meetings with kids?

Class meetings are source of providing information other than the academic or the subjects. It helps to deliver the social ethics and make an interactive atmosphere with the class mates and friends. Kids are open up about their emotions, feelings and issues. It is a source that facilitate the opportunity of problems solving. Teacher can make it more interesting by incorporating different activities, games or short quiz to improve the kid's engagement. As well as it is a source to educate them about manners and class ethics, it is an individual opportunity for every kid to grow and present the personality in an organized way.

Why family class meetings for preschoolers?

Teachers can engage the family of preschoolers in a class meeting. It is a source through which parents can have a check on their kid's activity and can know about the performance. As well as share the behavior of kid in a particular situation with the instructor so, he or she could better work by considering the things.

Benefits of class meetings

- Class meetings build an interactive and personal communication skills in you kids. In a multiple way it improves the personality and enhance the growth and development chances.
- Give ways to educate about self-controlling skills, emotions interpretation and expression of feelings.
- Can improve the skills of making friends and sharing things with each other
- Give a way to solve problems by easily diagnosing them
- It can enhance the sense of responsibility as well as create an emotional association with each other.

The World "Out There": Dealing with the Influence of Technology and Culture

Technology incorporation impact our living style and cultural values so much. According to the research it is evaluated that the technology has a strong and powerful impact on the culture. It totally modifies the living styles, learning habits, make life easier and due to its valuable impact has a significant role in our life. When we talk about the technology and its impact on the child learning and ethical approach it really worth. With the use of mobile, internet, computer you can access the multiple information online that provides a way out to work on the child learning and ethical training and growth more effectively. Like internet is fast changing thing it provides information of set of information that not only helpful in to do daily task as well as provide problem solving solutions in an effective manner.

Preschool learning and impact of technology

To an infant or a kid, you have to educate and train about multiple of things that can be ethical, health, protection and safety. Internet and technology make the information accessible easily and as a parent you can have expert tips to improve the overall health and safety of your kid. You can plan multiple interactive brain storming activities for the kids and make them to learn new things quickly.

Parenting and culture

As per the statistics it is recorded that different culture means parents with different perceptions. It depends on the culture to culture that how parents react and communicate with their children. Culture has a greater influence on the child behavior and interaction with the society. Kids usually follow the way of their parents and adopt the things from their behavior in response to the society impression. If parents one or both belongs to different culture groups, then we can see the great influence of each one's culture on the child. Child's behavior influence with the culture has a vast effect of the kid's development and personality growth. The language, ethics, manners and many more things that are directly influence by the culture where the kid is living and learning.

Technology and kids learning

No doubt technology is an effective thing that improve our daily life a lot. It helps in a multiple way to work better on the kids' education, grooming and leaning habits. Side by side technology has a bad and negative impact on the kid's personality. Too much the use of technology reduces the physical interaction and exercise that proves necessary for the physical development and mental grooming as well. For the infants, toddlers it is necessary to put them into physical activities as much as it is possible to improve their coordination, interactive capabilities and mental growth as well. But too much reliance on the technology not only have the negative behavioral impact but also health complications as well.

According to the studies and research it is noticed that the brain of a child is initially at the development process and if you just put them in front to technology the development may be affected by tech badly. As well as another study, ensure the exposure towards technology turn the growth of a kid brain like the quick scanning, processing and streaming the information multiple times.

It is good to introduce the kids to technology by incorporating the interactive learning sources and ways. Nevertheless, keep in mind the physical interaction like an old school of parenting did is a more effective source to educate the kids about ethical learning and basic health and caring tips that are useful for the life.

Chapter 7: When your Child Needs Special help

There are certain situations in life when you need to pay special attention to your kid. It is not necessary that you kid need the special attention only when he is with some special needs. A normal kid in his life needs some special attention in order to meet up the regular challenges. The core concept to understand is the need of such help in the normal routine as well.

Not all the kids are able to do everything with the same pace. At some point in their social and educational life, they need to do things differently. As parents it is necessary for you to identify when your kid need special attention and help from you.

The special help is not about accessing a hospital in case of not feeling well or approaching for an extra class to give better education. The help is about being at the back of your kid in any manner and make him feel comfortable about the situation. Giving a kid hope that everything is going to be fine and there is nothing to fear about in the world as far as the parents are there. Here are some situations when you need to be there with kids.

Unable to focus

If your kid is unable to focus on anything whether it is a practical demonstration or learning then you should get an idea of something happening wrong. May be the kid is not interested in the activity or exposed to some confusions or fears. You can help the kid in understanding the activity and help him to focus the situation without getting worried of anything else.

Having sleep issues

One of the core issues that kids have is in the bedtime. Sometimes they are feared of darkness, isolation or nightmares as well. In such situation, forcing the kid to sleep is not a good idea. You need to make him deal with the situation and fight back all the ideas and fears in his mind.

Health is not on a good note

When the kids are not feeling well they are in a vulnerable situation. They can react to the things differently all the time. Mood swings, anger, sadness all of these feelings can come up together or on interval basis. You need to understand the situation and help our child to overcome the fear or feeling of not being so well in that specific time.

Unable to express

Some kids are not good with expression. They do not have any idea about the selection of words or expressions to say what they feel. When there is a situation of unrest, you need to help the kid by understanding behaviors. At this time, you can rescue the kid by helping him in feeling comfortable to tell you what is cooking insides his mind.

Mixed feelings of anger, excitement and sorrow

One of the critical situations with a child is when he is unable to identify the real feeling. At this time, he behaves differently due to the mix emptions toward a happening or person. You need to help the kid about knowing that is happening to him and why. Moreover, you should help the kids to deal with such conditions efficiently.

Growing as a Family: Finding Support, Resources, and Sanity

Positive discipline is not about letting your kid learn all the things independently. It is not a kind of high school training where you kid needs to learn everything on his own. It is about a family, a home and all the peers together. If you want your kids to be healthy in body and mind as well, you need to grow as a family.

Family it not just about having food together, living in a house, going on vacations and all the good things. Family is there for anyone in the hard times and bad things as well. To encourage positive discipline in your kids it is necessary to make them understand the need and importance of the family. When you are good enough to maintain a good family system, you will be able to make things better.

A person craves for three things from his family, support, resources and sanity. All these three things have the integral importance in the overall learning of kids and their growth as well. The most important thing is to consider that without these three elements a family cannot have a healthy future.

Your support is the key

When you are teaching the kids about the positive discipline and way of life then you need to provide them complete support. There can be multiple behaviors on the go that your kid will express in the beginning. You are supposed to understand these actions, reactions and then support the kid accordingly. For his or her good, you need to understand the need and then as a family, you need to support them.

The issue can be anything; it can be a failure, a bad habit, some physical or psychological deficiency or any health issue as well. In all the phases, the support and shelter by the family in the right manner can help the kid to sustain the situation. The support to your kid in a critical situation is not that you are covering up the mistakes or giving an exit from something wrong. It is about making the kid understand about what's right and what makes things wrong as a whole.

Even if you kid has done something that is not right you need to make him realize the mistake and support him to make correction. On the other hand, if your kid is unable to learn new things then you need to adopt the things that can help him with a better understanding of the issue. This support of the family will increase your kid's reliance on family and he will look towards the family in any need or situation that demands support.

Hit the help resources

Finding the resources to help your kids and family is another important thing that makes a family. If there is something happened wrong, there is a fault line in your kids or a deficiency; you need to hit the right resources to help. These resources can be of personal, individual, family based and outsourced as well. You need to identify the appropriate resource as per the need.

Medical attention

Feeling unwell is one of the common problems faced by the kids. Anything new happens to them makes them feel sick. It is not about the real medical problem all the time but sometimes a change in hormone, conditions and brain activities. Sometimes, kids can be serious too. Medical changes are a kind of complex issue that can hit the kids badly. In such matters other than family support and condolence, medical attention and a professional help is necessary. Make sure to be with your kid all the time as it is necessary for him to have someone he can trust and really on. It can help the kid in not to panic.

Additional attention

Sometimes kids need additional or special attention when going through a feeling or phase. Mostly it happens in case of any loss, trauma or bad health. You need to use your attention as a resource and give the maximum attention and time to the kid. It will help him to get close to you and open to the issues and problems. The close relation can help to make things even better between the families and keep the unit connected.

Discussion and debate

Sometimes the perceptions about the problem are not good enough. You need to discuss and debate on the issue with the kids. In this moment, the kids can express what they actually feel and what are the real problems they have regarding a specific issue. This can actually help in making a real difference in the overall situation. As family, it is important to discuss issue, conflicts and problems with each other in a healthy environment.

Educational grooming

Sometimes there are behavioral issues that kids shown in certain situation. It is because they do not have any education about dealing with the situation. You need to invest time and look into the educational grooming of the child. It is about solving the problem he is having inside mind and make things even for the rest.

Getting study kits

If the child is unable to study well, then you can get him the study kits. These resources help a child to know things better. Using the simple and easy themes, these kits can breakdown the complex terms easily and let the kid know better and more. You need to select these kits carefully in order to get the right results.

Understand the variation

It is no necessary that all the kids are of same nature and have the same needs, behaviors and reactions to the things. If you kid is behaving differently than others it is necessary for you to know that everyone is different from each other. This variation is the beauty of the humankind. This difference makes a person capable of doing something different from the other do. To grow as a family you need to understand this concept of variation and take the further steps for improvement.

Explore the options

Other than support, resources and understanding there are multiple options you have to make your family stronger and kids table. Remember, it is not necessary that if you have a challenges kid only then you need to pay extra attention. For every kid there is a need to look around for the best options and get the right things in the box. Every single kid is different and you need to explore the options for all your kids differently. You cannot match all your three kids – if there are – with each other and expect them to behave the same way.

Here are some other practical things that you are supposed to consider and work on:

Match interests

Being a parent, you need to be the closest friends to your kids. It is only possible when you are sharing the same interests with them. It is not possible that the whole family will have the same interests but they can grow. As parents, you can set up some of the common habits for all the kids so everyone can have good time together. On the other hand, do not restrict any new interest of your kids. In fact, you can participate in the other activities with them so they can rely on you. It will help you kids so share what they feel and how they perceive the other things around. Moreover, you can help them grow better by knowing things better.

Participate to make it rational

If your kids are differently doing something because they are unable to do it the way others do then its fine. You do not have to be worried, instead of getting them out of their comfort zone you are supposed to make their zone comfort for themselves. As far as your kid is trying hard to be something, so you are supposed to help in with that. Your participation in the task can make this unique style rational and it will not make your kid feel awkward about it. Something with participation you can make your kid learn the right or rational way to do something. All you need is to observe, participate, and anticipate the problem.

Boost your kid's confidence

If you kid is doing something different that is not as per the specific gender or social roles for him. You are supposed to support him in every manner. It is important to boost his confidence with the best arguments and tools. You can make the kid feel normal about his diversity and do not make him answerable for the diversity in him. The actions of support can help him to be better with everything exclusive he holds in himself.

Make him realization of variation

Most of the kids are not confident and comfortable with their abilities or overall skills. They do not find themselves similar to others and this causes them to be in depression or face bad behavior. As a parent, you need to make your kid realize about the variation and make him understand the difference is always for good. It is not necessary that your kid will learn variation only he is different. Every kid needs to understand this important factor of variation so he or she can help the other mates at school, late in collage or workspace and eventually in society. This realization is the door and success pathway to a balanced and healthy lifestyle in future.

Learn the best way to deal with it

If a kid is having something exceptional, not normal, below average or anything, the best help is the realization and its handling. You need to let your kid learn about the tactics and treatments of the issue. It will help him to lead a balanced and confident life. For this purpose, you do have a number of resources already available out there. The best positive discipline is to make your kid able enough to lead his life independently in the coming years.

Chapter 8: Positive Discipline Solutions A-Z

Developing positive discipline in your children is not an easy and quick thing. It takes time and effort. Other the efforts you need to face a number of challenges and treat them. Your kids can display a number of reactions, problems and issues that needs a solution on priority. Here we got you some of the core issues and their solutions that can help you to make situation better.

Sibling rivalry

When a child is a single child, he is getting complete attention from the parents and everyone else. With the birth of second child, your first child start feeling ignored and all the love is now shared with the sibling. It causes a little pinch of sibling rivalry. It starts silently and gradually grows to the next level. In the positive discipline of your child, it is one of the major challenges that you need to encounter. To deal with it you need to make the elder child comfortable with the younger one and let them both develop a love bond of their own. It will help you to wipe off the rivalry feels from the story.

School problems

Going to school is a nightmare for your kids. It contains a fear of meeting new people, dealing with them or is bullied by teachers or other students. You need to prepare your kids mentally and physically to deal such fears. Make them understand the diversity of school, purpose of study and help them to manage the study pressure in their own manner. The management of homework and studies can play an integral role in solving their school problems.

Eating preferences

There is always a war on the dinging table. Parents know the nutrition and kids know the taste. It is totally in your hands; if you do not want your kid to eat; unhealthy you are supposed to quit it. Once you are not eating it, there is no other reference to introduce kids to the fancy meals. Additionally, to keep the kids stick to the house meals you can provide them variations of cuisines and good taste as well.

Tatting and Lying

Most of the parents are worried about the habits of lying and tatting in their kids. It is something that is not acceptable in positive discipline but it is hard for the kids to avoid it. If you want your kid not to lie then you need to understand the cause of it. Commonly, kids use to lie because they do not want to share something as they have fear of punishment. You need to make them understand that sharing the issue will not lead them to trouble but lie do. When they trust you, and freely share the things then you can help them in making things good and improved as a whole. It appears to be a suitable solution to the problem.

And more

The above mentioned and discussed problems are not the sole issues that you may have to face with your kids. There can be many other issues that can involve the physical and psychological challenges as well. It is important for you to know the right way out for the problems and issues kids are causing in the process.

Pro tip

The ultimate tip for the entire parent is to keep calm and then tackle the situation and issues in the first hand. It is not wise to get hyperactive or exhausted from the situation and let the kids make the ultimate unrest on their side. With a little observation and cool mind you can actually make a great difference in the situation.

Work On Magic Wands, Being Human, Reconnection & Change

In the positive discipline you need to work on a few things in general that includes fantasies, human realities, connecting generations and bringing change. All these things are interconnected in a process. We can say that the positive discipline is actually based on the steps that connects to each other and gets us the required results as well. Parents need to follow these steps in order to achieve the right results.

Magic wands

Our kids love to be in the fantasy zone and most of their cartons, storybooks and material is based on fantasy, magic and spells. As parents, you need to make them understand about the difference of reality and fiction. It will help them to know that the world outside is much different and challenging. It is the first step of parenting and positive discipline. We may find it easy to bring fictions for kids but this is somehow bringing kids away from reality.

Being human

The next big thing we want to achieve from the positive discipline is the humanity. The kids should feel the human inside instead of a machine. So many machines surround us these days that we do not have any world outside these things. The purpose is to bring the human side back to our kids so they can meet others, feel the paint, do something for good and welfare as well. By getting, those to social interaction and making kinds interact with each other can help them to be sensitizing about humankind.

Reconnection

Positive discipline actually reconnects kids to the roots and history as well. It is all about making a kid learn about how human beings communicate. It is about making them understand the man's connection with each other, nature, environment, society and others. The process actually make kids enable to understand diversity and accept it as it is.

Bringing change

The core purpose of positive discipline learning to the kids is to bring change in their lives. It helps them to leave the bas things like discrimination, hate, lies, fears, confusion, and isolation behind. They can learn how to communicate, socialize and deal with the people in society with the best grounds. Eventually the process can make a visible change in the lives of kids and society as well. There will be more acceptance, sharing, care, opportunities and positivity among the kids.

Conclusion

Training kids with positive discipline and giving them a perfect code of living is not an easy task at all. Every kid is different from the other and they have their own understanding of the events as well. although there are some set patterns defined that parents make kids learn. But, the self understating and evaluation of the matters cause a real difference in their understanding and practice. As parents, it is important to understand that all kids are different and have different needs or interests. You can make them learn some of the basic things like personal hygiene, mannerism, understanding or world order and basic behaviors in general. However, it is not possible to control their reactions, emotions, actions and understanding about everything that is around.

The make your kids grow better and help them with all the good things around it is necessary to understand their diversity. Additionally, it is necessary to understand how their needs are different from the others and it is fine to be different. You need to support them in order to construct a better and balanced personality. Imposing the interests and career selections can never be a good option for your kid's brain development.

There should be mutual interests and consultation but a liberty of selection. Your kids need ultimate help from you in the hard times. Their attitude and behavior ask you to look at them and ask the matter not to just punish and put them to detention. A process starts with the beginning and prolong until death. You can identify the important needs of your child and evaluate when, how you can help them with the question, issues, and problems they have. Additionally you can reconnect them to the humankind and reality of life by cutting them off from the imaginary world of cartoons. Overall, your combined efforts of good food, lifestyle, education, time, money and support can lead the kids to positive discipline in life.

www.ingramcontent.com/pod-product-compliance
Lightning Source LLC
Chambersburg PA
CBHW021428070526
44577CB00001B/112